I have seen the saddest threadbare remnants of a bear and have felt his soul, alive and reaching.

Jama Kim Rattigan

Copyright © 1996 by Running Press.
Illustrations copyright © 1996 by Joan Gallup
All rights reserved under the Pan-American and International Copyright Conventions.

This book may not be reproduced in whole or in part, in any form or by any means,
electronic or mechanical, including photocopying, recording, or by any information storage
and retrieval system now known or hereafter invented, without written permission from the publisher.

9 8 7 6 5 4 3 2 1
Digit on the right indicates the number of this printing.

ISBN 1-56138-698-7

Designed by Frances J. Soo Ping Chow
Edited by Tara Ann McFadden
Printed in the United States

This book may be ordered by mail from the publisher.
Please add $2.50 for postage and handling.
But try your bookstore first!

Running Press Book Publishers
125 South Twenty-second Street
Philadelphia, Pennsylvania 19103-4399

Teddy Bear Journal

an illustrated notebook

RUNNING PRESS
PHILADELPHIA · LONDON

Hug a teddy bear in the evening, and you can feel him hugging back all the next day.

Tam Mossman

Prescription for relief of tears and nervous tension: one teddy bear, taken as needed. No side effects, but the love may become addictive.

James D. Nelson

Cuddly and warm, these calming creatures reassure me in the days of doubt when fears fly before reason and the world looms bleak instead of beautiful. The teddy bear, all things to all ages, all sizes for all preferences, symbol that all is right with the world if one only believes.

Anonymous

We have to show the world that it's not unmanly to have a teddy bear.
George B. Black Jr.

I read where the teddy bear is "a symbol used by people of all ages to recapture infant security in the face of frightening new situations." I don't know; I just feel better having him around.

Edward McGettigan

People believe in teddy bears because teddy bears believe in people. Teddies count on people to get them down off of toy shelves and into human arms.

Kathy Cressman

Teddy bears have always seemed to me to be, above all other toys, the symbol of loving-kindness.

Lesley Blanch

There are as many kinds of teddy bears as there are people.
John Blackburn

A bear that's going to sit and watch a football game with you isn't going to carry himself the same way as a bear who just sits on a shelf.

Irene Heckel

Everyone has a teddy bear secret.

Anonymous

Long before I grew up, my teddy bear taught me what love really meant—being there when you're needed.

Jim Nelson

You can name a teddy bear anything from "Eurastis" to plain old "Cat," and he won't even mind if you keep changing it.

Karri Anne Schniering

Big bears are good for sleeping with, for crying on. . . .
Little bears are intimate. They are portable. They can be
ready at a moment's notice for unobtrusive travel and companionship, solace and the sharing of secrets.

Carol-Lynn Rössel Waugh

Bears make strangers into bedfellows.
Eloise Coopersmith

Parents and others are very arbitrary in deciding when a child should stop having his or her teddy bear around. My mother thought sixteen was about the right time. I still think she was wrong and I'm sure Theodore agrees with me.

Peter Bull

The way my parents got my older sister to give up her teddy was to persuade her that I needed him more. As it turned out, I did.

Wendy Walker

I can see a world without lots of things, but I can't see a world without teddy bears.

Harry Nizamian

The more I learned about teddy bears the more mysterious their enormous appeal became. "Why bears, why not cats or elephants?" the curious-minded ask. "Why indeed!" huffs any true teddy bear lover, "everyone knows why teddy bears are special."

Carolyn Vosburg Hall

You just can't win a staring contest with a teddy bear.

Tom Armstrong

Bears are irresistible because all people are kids. Grown-ups are just kids who have been around for a while (quite a while in some cases).

Kathy Cressman

Wherever the boy went, there was teddy. Where teddy was, there was the boy. And, every night they'd sleep together, curled as tight as two pieces of a jigsaw puzzle, keeping one another warm.

George E. Murphy Jr.

Nothing satisfies like a good bear hug.
Marianne Pontician

Nighttime is the best time to have a friend like a bear.
Carol-Lynn Rossell Waugh

I was pushing my cart down the grocery store aisle, mind focused on bananas and boxed cereal, when I was distracted by a shelf of teddy bears. One seemed to be reaching out to me. I checked my shopping list, but there were no "Bears" written down. I try to avoid impulse buying, and started on down the aisle. I guess I needed that bear, because I wheeled my cart around, and in he went, sitting happily on a head of lettuce.

Molly Courville

Old teddy bears are filled with excelsior, love, and warm memories.
Wanda Loukides

. . . above all, he is jointed, which makes him automatically an intelligent listener.

Peter Bull

There is a touch of sadness that endears bears to me, like layers of peeling paint on a beautiful old building. And there is a bear smell—musty, old, and dry. It's the smell of an attic on a hot afternoon. Only good things that have lasted have that smell—trunks, and lace and blankets.

Michele Durkson Clise

Teddies are father figures. To children they represent goodness, benevolence, and kindliness. Parents who replace this cozy unharmful toy are a menace.

Joshua Bierer

So perfectly in his grizzly exterior adapted to fitting into the many chubby arms which are extended for him.

Caroline Ticknor

Teddy bears may fade, sag, stain, or shed, but their personalities are never affected. They just go on being perfect.

Peggy and Alan Bialosky

My parents never forbad me my teddy bear; I have one yet. But what they did do was replace my old, worn-out cotton and wool bear with a sanitized nylon version. To this day, I have an ingrained aversion to change of any sort.

Michael Callaghan

If the bear is missing an eye, and you can't find a replacement, make an eye patch, and your bear will look swashbuckling. If it is missing a paw or an arm, make a plaster cast and tell folks the arm was broken in a skiing accident.

Peggy Bialosky

My teddy was there when I had no friends to play with, no one to talk to, no one to share my little woes or my big joys. He looked constant and was constant. He never aged, no matter how tattered he became. His smell was the smell of my years as a boy, and he alone knew everything. Now, when I see him on the shelf, he is like my flesh and my soul—older, worn, but still full of happiness.

Robert Kunciov

He's thirty years old now, passed down from my mother. . . .
Now my problems are more complicated, but still he learns.

Claudia Stahl

My teddy bear is faceless, short of fur and stuffing;
but his bravery protects me from the shadows of the night.

Jean Van de Zande

Love breeds teddy bears and teddy bears breed love!

Wendy L. Harrod

Why do people love teddy bears? It's for their don'ts . . . they don't eat your food, they don't dance with your date, and they don't trump your ace lead.

Jim Davis

For most . . . Teddies provide companionship. Their suitability for dressing up and investing with personalities, and their endearing facial expressions, have often led to Teddies becoming honorary family members.

Pauline Cockrill

Nonsense is the *whole point* of teddy bears! Teddy bears give us a chance to be silly. Silliness is a very important part of life. Being silly is as refreshing as meditation, exercise, or group therapy. And Teddies bring out our natural silliness.

Barbara Wolters

Teddy bears sit around the tea table at mealtimes, play games, entertain at parties, work at domestic duties such as cooking, cleaning, and repairing. Fortunately, whatever the activity, whether at work or play, they seem to be in a state of perpetual enjoyment.

Deborah Stratton

Where is he now? I don't know.
He got lost in the shuffle of what is
called the growing-up process, but
he never stopped following me, and
sometimes when I thoughtfully
look back, there he is, looking at
me with that surprised expression
that says, "Hi! How y' doing?"

Marcus Bach

It is not just in the nursery that the symbol of the bear has prominence. In the heavens too, the bear reigns supreme.

Giorgio Coppin

Teddy bears make great confessors, advisors, best friends—and scapegoats. Whenever my mother prepared to punish me for one misdeed or another, I would always be ready with "Teddy did it!"

Anonymous

Love and loyalty are the bear essentials.
Marianne Pontician

Once you buy a bear with a wonderful expression, you're hooked for life. It's like a blood disease—a delightful one.

Don Groves

They're good listeners and gentle talkers, who don't say anything too profound except "I love you."

Arthur Woodstone

Posession of a teddy bear after a certain age
is a very private matter indeed.
Peter Bull